The Trees
With No Leaves

The Trees With No Leaves

BY

GREER ALEXIS BACON

Dedication

To David, when I wrote this story 10 years earlier before meeting you. It was only a dream of seeing the beauty of nature. I never would imagine it would be our back yard someday.

The Trees
With No Leaves

In the deep foothills of the Black Forest, rich in natural beauty, a boy named Hans lived with his father and mother. They were a simple family with an ordinary routine. As a child, Hans became quite good at being a handyman with his father. Each summer when school let out Hans helped his father gather wood in the forest.

They worked together from the moment the sun arose until its slow descent at the early evening. Hans was well suited for the physically challenging days. One by one, Hans helped his father to bundle wood for the coming fall and winter. The whistle of the trees could be heard at least a mile way.

Hans knew that all this work would be well rewarded with a cozy fireplace when the chill of winter came knocking at the door each year. Folktales were commonly known around the Black

Forest. Nothing interested Hans more than the tale of the trees with no leaves.

It was a challenge to believe that such folk tales could possibly be true. But Hans still wondered and kept a lookout each season.

During Han's eighteenth year his father grew ill and wasn't able to collect wood that summer. Hans was well prepared to take on his duty, which he did with no trouble. Each day was the same as before. Cut, chop and gather. The Black Forest was peaceful. The sun glared through the evergreen trunks and reflected on the forest ground with life.

Hans was busy loading the back wagon with wood. Steel Gray, Han's horse, was hitched to the wagon. He was a lovely grey horse with a long black mane. Suddenly a wind caused a bunch of unsettled dead leaves that rested at the edge of the wagon's wheels to blow away.

Hans looked up and saw the fast approaching storm coming straight for them. He knew he couldn't make it back home before the storm hit. He quickly grabbed Steel Gray's strap and looked for safety deep in the forest. It was so dense; the sky became smaller and smaller as he looked up through the trees. The rain began to fall. Deeper and deeper he went until he noticed an odd opening with a center pin of light.

"Over there, Steel," Hans said. He unhitched the wagon from his horse and they made their way into a hidden cave. The cave was covered in bush. The rain poured like buckets; the sunny day, had changed in a moment. Hans and Steel Gray waited until the storm had passed and Hans could see the sun trying to peek through the forest.

At the back of the cave Hans noticed a tiny light

that had not been there before. He wondered to himself, *What can that be?* He slowly pulled Steel Gray beside him and walked towards the light.

The light become more and more rich with colors and the hole became larger and larger in size. Hans couldn't believe his young eyes. Could this be? It was the most magical sight he could have ever imagination.

He and Steel Gray were standing at the foothills of the where the trees stood. There was not a leaf in sight. The rich warm sun brought life to this magical moment. There were no leaves on the tips of the branches of any of these trees, only butterflies. One by one they started stretching their wings and within a moment they released themselves into the warm air.

It was breath taking to Hans. The butterflies

landed on him and Steel Gray, and then, suddenly, they were gone. Where they went was a mystery. But the folk tale was true!

That afternoon Hans shared his story with his parents with excitement. To prove to his parents that the tale was true, Hans encouraged them to join him for a ride to see it for themselves. But to his surprise, although he clearly remembered the route to the cave, it was nowhere to be found. Disappointed, he sadly made his way back home with them.

As the years passed, Hans told his story of that magical day in the forest with Steel Gray to each one of his own children and his wife, yet all refused to believe that such beauty could exist.

Anna, Hans' youngest granddaughter, was six years old. She, too, listened to the tales of her

grandpa. Her favorite story was the one of pretty little butterflies.

Late one summer evening, around Anna's bedtime, the whole family was joyfully sitting on the front porch. Anna approach her grandpa. With a little voice, she whispered in his ear. " I believe you, Grandpa."

Hans grinned from ear to ear. "I shall take you there."

The next morning, Hans helped Anna put on her shoes. Holding onto her hand, he slowly guided Anna through the thick, dense forest. Before long, behold, the cave that was impossible to find stood as clear as day in front of them!

"See, Grandpa, I told you so."

"What, Anna?"

"I believe you. That's why I can see."

Through the cave to the opening light, as still as the flowers at their feet, stood the trees with no leaves, but only butterflies.

As we stood there, Anna and I, I realized that the beauty of seeing was the beauty of believing. As the butterflies left one by one in the far distant sky, Anna and I waved goodbye.

THE END

About the Author

"Stand up for what you believe in even if it means standing alone..."
— C.M.

Greer with her three year old Daughter Honor

GREER ALEXIS BACON, a native of Westchester NY. Today, Lives in the Finger Lakes Region of Western NY. Where she and her husband raise their two children and work full time. Greer has been writing since 2001 where she

15

started with poetry. Then not until 2005, Greer started working on "Guardian, Where A Dream Is Challenged" her first published work. Today, she continues to write children's books. Stories that will touch children's heart as well adults alike. With help, to bring her books alive, T.D Smartgroupvn an artist from Vietnam. He illustrates each picture with the beauty of watercolor paints. Greer would love to hear from her fans like you! You can email her at: greerbacon@gmail.com

To many years of reading and writing,

Greer Alexis Bacon

www.ingramcontent.com/pod-product-compliance
Lightning Source LLC
Chambersburg PA
CBHW050933290526
45792CB00002B/999